MW01064965

I Want You to Call Him Tyler

Stephanie L. King

A story of uncommon cruelty - how it was conquered with love and forgiveness.

Stephanie L. King

Copyright © 2013 Stephanie L. King

ISBN-13: 978-1481003629
ISBN-10 1481003623

This book is dedicated to the following people:

Pat Emmons. This is the man who saved Tyler's life. He rescued Tyler after July 4th and brought him to the Small Animal Clinic.

Dr. Annette Baker and staff, Small Animal Clinic. Without their help, Tyler would not have survived.

Jack Acklin, Retired FBI Special Agent, who encouraged me to write this book. Jack attends their monthly luncheons and always asks, "Hey, Stef, how is our dog and the writing of 'our' book coming along?"

ACKNOWLEDGEMENTS

Linda Hight is the editor of this book. She is also the wife of a retired FBI Agent and volunteered her services last year at our annual retired Agents Christmas dinner. As we were both former employees of the FBI and married to retired Agents, we immediately had a bond. Since that time, we have become great friends. She introduced me to her Walking Buddies and I am now a happy member of that group.

Thank you, Linda, so much for your help, time and attention to the details that I knew nothing about. Linda also advised on the publishing and marketing of this book. You are the best.

Frank King, my husband of 45 years, who typed and advised on editing, changes and insights that has been invaluable to me. Since he loves the computer and I do not, I have let him do everything after I wrote the book in longhand. Thank you, honey.

CONTENTS

LIFE AS WE KNEW IT

Once upon a time………………..all the best stories of our lives seem to start that way and this one certainly qualifies. For us, it was just after the 4th of July, 2008 and my husband and I were going to have our lives changed dramatically. Little did we know that not only our lives, but our minds and our very hearts were all just waiting to be touched and warmed. We were going to be "found" by one of God's creatures who would not only teach us about total acceptance, but he would show us an amazing ability to forgive and, above all else, to love.

We were not "found" in any normal or routine way and I must say, I was not planning to own a pet. My husband and I were born during WWII. My father was in the U.S. Navy and I was the oldest of four children. We lived in many places and each time as our family grew, it was not possible to have pets. At one point in time we had a dog as our family pet.

During one of our moves, we were forced to leave this dog behind. This pet was mine and I missed her and grieved for years.

Eventually, when we were settled, we were able to have dogs. My whole family has always loved dogs and among all of us, there have probably been at least twenty dogs at various times in our lives. My husband and I had a dog for twelve and a half years. She was a dachshund and we had her from the age of two years until her death at twelve and a half years old. Her name was Pretzel and she was definitely my dog. It fell to me to have her put to sleep when her time had come. It was horrible for me and I swore I would never have another dog because the end of their story is just too painful for me. When she passed away, we never got another pet.

"Blessed is the person who has earned the love of an old dog."

Stephanie L King

The Journey of Lost

All the Way to Found

My husband, Frank, a retired FBI Agent, and a few other retired Agents were patrolling an area of underground natural gas storage fields. The fields were owned by a major natural gas company in northeastern Oklahoma and the surveillance was in place twenty-four hours a day, seven days a week. The company had experienced some pilfering of their products in a rural area not far from where we live. The nature of this request required surveillance of an area that was approximately two and a half miles in circumference. This required an hourly check of the area to look for any suspicious behavior. This surveillance project lasted from March to October of 2008.

In 2008, the 4th of July occurred on a Friday. Several times during surveillance, the men would see two dogs running loose down in a creek bed and among a heavy overgrowth of weeds. When these dogs heard a car coming, they would come up to the road and greet the person in the car and then come around to the passenger side as if they wanted inside the car.

The dogs appeared to have been well cared for and the assumption was they had been "dumped" in the area. It seemed as if they were just waiting for their owners to come back, hence they checked each car they heard, thinking it might be their owners and did not stray from this location.

On most days, when Frank completed his surveillance shift, he would come home and tell me about these dogs. He would plead with me to bring them home with him. After losing Pretzel, you can understand my hesitation. I kept giving Frank excuses. First, I told him absolutely not because it would tie us down too much. I thought that having two dogs when we were enjoying life as it was, would just complicate our lives. With my memories of Pretzel and the pain of losing her, you can better understand why the battle was raging within my heart about saying 'yes' to having another dog. However, God had other plans.

After that 4th of July weekend, on the following Monday, Pat Emmons, who worked many of the midnight shifts, arrived at the creek bed area and found the younger of the two dogs lying on the side of the road. This young pup was bleeding from his mouth and appeared to be lifeless. The other dog, thought to be a mother or father, was nowhere in the area and was never seen again. Pat, a dog lover and owner, with a tender heart, bundled the injured dog into his car. It was around 7:00 am and he was trying to find a vet on the way home. At that time of morning, he wondered if a veterinary would even be open. The first veterinary clinic he found was closed and he continued to look for one that opened early. As he continued his search, he found the Small Animal Clinic which, thankfully, was open. It is owned and operated by Dr. Annette Baker. Pat talked to Dr. Baker and explained the circumstances as to how he came to have the dog. He left the dog there and gave them some money to do whatever was necessary for this small dog, to include euthanizing him if need be. It became a personal challenge for Dr. Baker and she made the decision to do everything in her power to bring the dog back from almost certain death. In her assessment, this dog was within a day or even hours from death.

The dog was x-rayed and no signs of gangrene were found. Dr. Baker checked the dog meticulously for other injuries. Her conclusion was that someone had intentionally harmed this dog. As hard as it is to imagine, she said it seemed that a substantial amount of fireworks (possibly a cherry bomb) had been put in the dog's mouth. This was ignited and caused extensive damage to the dog's teeth, his lower jaw and his tongue. The x-rays revealed three upper teeth on the right side of his mouth were missing as well as a portion of his lower jaw. There was also a portion of the back of his tongue that was missing. The x-ray showed fragments of teeth and bone having been blown into the muscle and tissues of his neck. Dr. Baker determined that these fragments were not sufficiently close to his spinal column and that they would remain in their current positions, which would negate any attempts at surgically removing any of these fragments which might have caused additional damage. These fragments would remain in place with virtually no chance of moving for the rest of his life.

Dr. Baker wired his jaw closed and used a special type of glue that allowed the jaw to heal properly. During his healing process, he was unable to fully open his mouth so the staff had to spoon feed him liquid foods by blending them.

Dogs laugh, but they laugh with their tails. ~Max Eastman, Enjoyment of Laughter

THE CLINIC THAT

CARED....AND

CARED....AND CARED.

The words of Dr. Annette Baker of the Small Animal

Clinic

The smell of dead flesh filled our clinic's air by the time I got to work on July 7th, 2008. I expected a busy day. It always is after a holiday. It seems that some people hold onto their pet emergencies until a regular day to avoid paying emergency prices.

A man, Pat Emmons, had dropped the black puppy off as soon as our door opened that morning. He found the puppy by a well site. The other dog that had been there was assumed to have been a parent, was never seen again. The original owners had abandoned the dogs along the oil field road. The well overseers fed the starving dogs part of their sandwiches when they went past the area during their work day. The little dog was hurting.

We finally anesthetized him at 5:00 pm, after having repeatedly peeked into his kennel all day to check that he was still alive. His eyes were glassy with a terrified look in them and his mouth was drooling saliva and blood. His X-rays showed teeth broken out of his lower jaw and shards of those teeth had been planted in his neck muscles. There was a half-moon sized wound blown out of his tongue, near his throat.   No wonder he only drank water all day long.

We wired his jaw back together and sutured the edges of his tongue. His tongue looks like someone took a bite out of the side. That night, we cleaned him up and waited until he woke up from the anesthesia. We kept him warm with microwaved rice socks and warm towels. Massive doses of antibiotics were given.

Why would anybody feed firecrackers or something worse to a dog?

He was awake and alert the next day. He could lap up gruel that we made from canned dog food and warm water. He took his medicine and after a couple of days, the rotten smell went away. For eight weeks, we fed and cared for him while his jaw healed. We all fell in love with our little "Underdog." He grew, he played, and he followed us around the office. We made him a small bed under the desk and he helped us run the office.

As word got out about our little puppy, people started calling and coming by to see him. Pat came to check on him. Mr. King also came by to visit. Our drug reps asked about him and even Carol Lambert from a local news channel came for an interview and to film him - just in case he needed a home. Donations were given to help the little fellow get well.

At nine weeks after the wiring, once again he was anesthetized and the wires holding his jaw bones together were snipped and removed. The tissue over the bone was sutured back together and more healing had to take place. He still ate gruel, but gradually he could chew, not just lap up the food.

One busy day we looked for him and found he had "filed" himself in the blue plastic file folder basket, under the desk. The basket was small and the puppy too big, but he was perfectly comfortable in that basket.

Eventually, he was well. He got his shots, was neutered and it was time to go to his new home. Frank and Stephanie wanted him so badly. They had not had a family dog for seventeen years, but they were fully invested in this little Underdog's life and his trials. He went home with them and we were sad to see him go, but happy for his great future. They bring him to our office for visits often; he expects cheese crackers and a visit to the backyard. He kisses Amanda and comes to me for hugs. The funny thing is, he loves everybody and he has no fear of strangers. After all he has lived through, he still Loves people. He is a lesson to us all of forgiveness.

Dogs are not our whole life, but they make our lives whole.

Roger Caras

TYLER'S X-RAYS

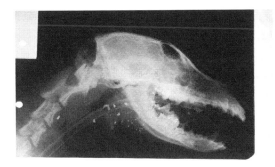

These x-rays show the pieces of his teeth and jaw bone were blown into his neck.

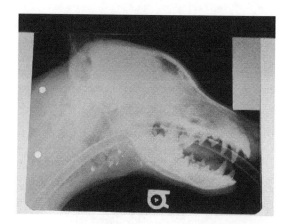

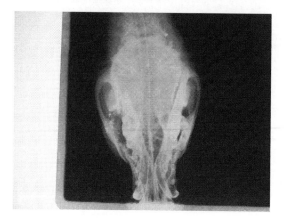

THIS IS THE FILE FOLDER BOX THAT BECAME TYLER'S FAVORITE PLACE AT THE SMALL ANIMAL CLINIC

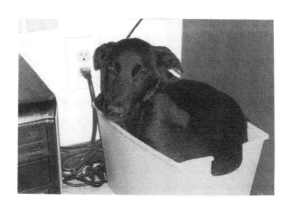

Happiness is a warm puppy. ~Charles M. Schulz

WHEN OUR HEARTS MET

FOR THE VERY FIRST TIME

In the early weeks while Dr. Baker cared for him, some of the Agents would visit and leave money for his treatment. It was during this time that Frank started his campaign to get me to the vet's office and to visit this puppy. Thinking back, I resisted for a couple of weeks before I gave in. One day, my daughter-in-law, Laura, was with me and I decided to finally go and visit the puppy I had heard so much about. The two of us joined Frank for our "formal introduction."

Laura, Frank, and I went in to the Small Animal Clinic. We were invited to come around behind the reception desk. There was another chair behind the desk next to the receptionist and I sat down. I looked under her desk and saw this little black puppy about six or seven months old, curled up in a basket. He looked directly at me with pleading brown eyes as if to say, "Ah-h-h-h. You're the one. I've been waiting for you."

He weakly got out of the basket and came directly over to me and nosed me. He then turned around and got back into the basket. I thought my heart would burst with love.

Whoever said you can't buy happiness forgot little puppies.

 ~Gene Hill

Stephanie L King

WHY WE CALL HIM

TYLER

A few days later after I had been introduced to this heart-warming black puppy, I was driving on a main street in our town when something happened that I will never forget. Not thinking of anything particular, I was minding my own business, just driving down the street. I glanced upward to a billboard with a lawyer's name on it. The last name was "Tyler." It was at that moment that I heard the Lord very clearly speak to me: "I want you to call him Tyler." Now as a Christian of many, many years, I am used to hearing the Lord's voice when He speaks to me (John 10: 27). If there had been any hesitation or doubt on my part as to whether we should adopt the dog, it was all dispelled at that moment!

Up to that point, we had not even talked to Dr. Baker about adopting him once he had recovered because I was still dragging my feet. No more - once the Lord said what He did, I knew what we had to do.

There is no faith which has never yet been broken, except that of a truly faithful dog. ~Konrad Lorenz

FROM UNDERDOG TO

WONDERDOG

The ladies who worked at the Small Animal Clinic had originally named the dog "Underdog," but once he began to recover and they saw his strength and his wonderful personality, they changed it to Wonderdog. So Wonderdog was still his name when the daughter of Pat Emmons mentioned this story to a local news channel. They wanted to interview Dr. Baker and "Wonderdog" about the abuse to him and his amazing recovery. We were able to record the segment and it still remains one our favorites to view again and again.

The interview opened with the female reporter asking Dr. Baker to tell the story about the dog. Wonderdog was sitting on the metal surgical table and Pat and Dr. Baker were standing close by during the filming.   Dr. Baker told the story and as much as she knew about the abuse. She mentioned that it was a terrible time of year for abuse to animals and how Pat had saved the dog from certain death. The x-ray showing the fragments in the dog's neck was also part of the filming of this story. The x-ray photos are also included in this book.

Up to this point, we had told Dr. Baker we would like to be considered as potential candidates for adopting Wonderdog. I did not say anything about what the Lord had said about naming the dog. So, at the end of the TV interview, Dr. Baker said, "Please, don't call the office about the dog because he's already spoken for." So as Frank and I were standing and watching the TV, we knew she meant he was ours!!

Pat Emmons really wanted to take Tyler, but already owned a dog and lived in an apartment that did not allow multiple pets.

In an awful twist of fate, two weeks after the local TV interview, Pat had a heart attack and passed away. One of his last acts of kindness was to save this dog from certain death. He is one of the people to whom this book is dedicated.

You think dogs will not be in heaven? I tell you, they will be there long before any of us. ~Robert Louis Stevenson

TYLER ARRIVES

AT HIS FOREVER

HOME

The next day we hurried to the vet and told her that we were going to name him "Tyler." He was not yet at the point that he could leave the vet's care so we were unable to take him home that day. Before we left though, a piece of masking tape was placed on his head so everyone would know to begin calling him "Tyler."

Finally, on September 11, 2008, we were able to bring Tyler to his new home. It had been almost exactly two months from the time he was rescued. Upon arriving home, Tyler explored everything and everywhere. He was a wonderful puppy with a precious temperament.

We began to wonder about the type of breed he was and what we might expect as he grew to adulthood. The only obvious breed we could see in him was that of a black Labrador retriever with very fine features, leading us to believe there was some kind of herding breed in him. Frank describes Tyler as being a "miniature" black lab.

When Tyler was brought into the vet's office, he weighed 21 pounds. After two months under their special care, he weighed around 40 pounds. Today, he is maintaining around 50 pounds.

"To err is human, to <u>forgive</u>, canine."

- Unknown

HOME IS WHERE

THE DOG IS

In thinking about the abusive things that were done to Tyler, one would have to conclude that he might be a mean dog. In addition to the damage done to his jaw, teeth and his tongue, his tail was cut off and remains approximately six inches in length which leads us to more evidence of abuse. Tyler's obvious appearance of being part black lab would indicate that he should have a normal tail. That does not stop him from wagging it excitedly. In light of this abuse, I have never known nor had a dog like him. He is utterly without malice toward any humans or other dogs. He does take great exception to squirrels and rabbits! When he is approached by a dog who acts aggressively, Tyler does not defend himself, he just sits down.

From the very beginning, all he ever wanted to do was please us. He learned very quickly what he could and could not do and what we thought was acceptable. Dr. Baker told us that rescued dogs make great pets because they have such an appreciation for having been rescued from abusive owners. Tyler's two month long stay with Dr. Baker and her staff had such a positive effect on Tyler.

Those ladies heaped great amounts of love on Tyler and we continue to reap the benefits of that love to this day.

When we first brought him home, he was very reluctant for us to pet his lower back near his tail. He would flinch or look back at us, as if to say, "Hands off my tail. That is not acceptable." As time has passed, we have won his trust and can pet him all over. He has total confidence in our love for him.

To further prove this point, he willingly and excitedly goes regularly to see Dr. Baker. She can do any kind of examination and he tolerates it all with no problems. In fact, I need to mention how crazy excited he gets when we tell him, "Let's go see Dr. Baker." He dances all over the place. How many dogs get excited about going to the vet?

Once there, he charges up to the reception desk and plants his feet on the ledge. Then, because he knows the drill, he goes to the large, flat scale for dogs and sits down, but only long enough for us to see his weight and give it to the receptionist. He then waits impatiently for Amanda, to come out and greet him.

Of course, Dr. Baker and Amanda remain his favorites as they cared for him for the two months he was healing. They are still with the clinic. During one of Tyler's recent visits to see Dr. Baker, she said, "I don't ever expect to find anything wrong with him because he has already paid his dues."

In fact, everytime we refer to Dr. Baker and Tyler is within hearing distance, we have to refer to her by using the initials, D R B, so he has no idea what we are saying. Otherwise, he will come running into the room wanting to know when we leave to go see her.

His absolutely delightful, loving, happy nature tells us that all he wants to do in life is to love us and make us happy. He always has a smile on his face with a look of constant anticipation of what's going to happen next!

How could anyone be so cruel to him and totally miss out on the wonderful blessing he really is. How could anyone look into those golden brown eyes and still be able to cut off his tail and leave him on a back road to die?

We have always wondered and asked ourselves about the other dog. What happened to it? Frank and the others presumed the dog might have been his mother or father.

About eighteen months after his rescue, Tyler, Frank and I traveled to where Tyler was found by the creek. As we approached the area, Tyler stood in the back seat dead still. We were on the side of the road where he and the other dog had been living.

We could tell he was profoundly affected by it. Not knowing how a dog thinks, anyone could see something very cathartic was taking place and that is why we did it - to let him know we knew.

"I think dogs are the most
amazing creatures; they give
__unconditional love__. For me they
are the role model for being alive."
- Gilda Radner

LIFE WITH

TYLER

To say that Tyler has been a blessing in our lives is an understatement. In my lifetime of having dogs, my family had, among others, three German Shepherds. Frank's family also had three German Shepherds. We are both in agreement that Tyler has greater intelligence than any of the six German Shepherds which says quite a lot since German Shepherds are such an intelligent breed.

When he first came to live with us, he would not voluntarily get into the truck or car. We had to pick him up and put him into the vehicle. As Tyler grew and became heavier, it was much harder to get him into either vehicle. The solution came when it dawned on Tyler that if I got into the truck and closed my door, I would be leaving. Being a dog of great intelligence, he realized he would be left behind once that door of mine closed. He immediately decided he could jump into the truck unassisted. He now jumps in and out with ease, as if it was all his idea in the first place.

Our next obstacle was to train him on the leash – oh, really? We had no idea that he strongly disliked the leash. Perhaps he had never been on a leash.

Possibly, he had been abused while attached to a leash. We tried countless times to teach him to walk on a leash. Finally, I had an idea that involved a timing change and thought it might work. We took him to a park and attached the leash before he jumped out of the vehicle. Absolutely no problem! Why it made a difference when we attached the leash will never be known. However, by changing that, it made a difference to Tyler. He had his first long range walk and loves it to this day.

Tyler, as most dogs, lives for his walks, so I walk him in the morning and evening. It is uncanny how he knows when it is time to walk. He goes into my closet and goes to my walking shoes to tell me it is time to go. When he meets other dogs along the way, he is always friendly, but is shocked if the other dog doesn't return those feelings. If another dog is aggressive, he seems to be totally surprised. All he wants to do is play and be friends. There is not an ounce of ALPHA male in him. He is the true meaning of being a lover, not a fighter.

"No matter how little money and
how few possessions you own,
having a dog makes you rich."
- Louis Sabin

TYLER KNOWS

One night I had the surprise of my life when Tyler went out for his regular evening outing before bedtime. There was a light on the roof of a guard house that is located at the back edge of our backyard. Tyler raced over to the corner of the yard by the guard house and started barking and looking up. There was a man on the roof who stated he was the owner of the company that had been hired to replace the roof on some of the common structures in our development. He was taking final measurements before starting work the next day. Tyler was dancing all around and continued his barking.

The man got off the roof and stood on the other side of our fence. He began petting Tyler and talking to him, so Tyler relaxed.

A few days later, the doorbell rang in the afternoon. Tyler ran barking to the front door as he usually does. He seems to be so excited that someone has come to visit him! When I opened the door, the man from earlier in the week wanted to speak to Frank as Frank was on the Homeowners Association Board of Directors. In the meantime,

Tyler blew past him and out into the yard. Tyler's hair was standing up and he was barking ferociously!

As I walked further outside, I could see another man in the yard who, due to the weather, was dressed in a heavy coat with the collar turned up and a large hat. Tyler had never seen this man before and he presented a threatening appearance to a dog that is very protective. Even though I had no assurance that this man was harmless, the only thing I could think to say to Tyler was, "Say hi to the nice man." Instantly, Tyler's hair went flat on his neck and he started doing his happy dance around this man.

I am thinking to myself, "I have never used that phrase with him before. How could he possibly know what I said or what it meant?" Tyler has an uncommon ability to "read" a person and to know by your tone of voice how he should react.

Many incidents since then with different people who have come to our front door, including yard workers, postal workers or sales people have brought the same results every time!

It is fascinating to watch his powers of deduction working and then to see him come to his own conclusions. When Tyler is told to do something, he will look at you, stand there for a second and then obey the order.

"Dogs have given us their absolute all. We are the center of their universe. We are the focus of their love and faith and trust. They serve us in return for scraps. It is without a doubt the best deal man has ever made."

- Roger Caras

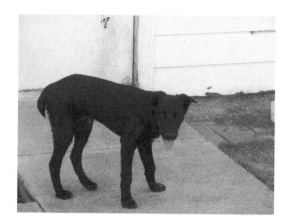

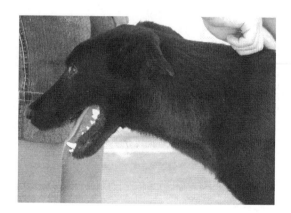

Stephanie L King

I Want You To Call Him Tyler

I Want You To Call Him Tyler

TRAINING

TYLER

(OR MAYBE

TYLER TRAINED ME!)

We have about eight locations where we like to take Tyler for walks. We use a retractable leash on him and it works better than any other leash we have tried. During one of his training sessions, I wanted to see if I could devise a way to keep him from getting tangled up and wrapped around things like poles, trees and bushes that would be between him and me as we walked. I had never been able to remedy this entanglement problem with any other dog. However, I had never used a retractable leash before so I started with the phrase, "This side." I would stop the leash until he came back around to my side. It took only a couple of walks before he totally understood what I meant. Now, when we are out walking and he is on one side and I am on the other of a vertical object, he stops and comes around to my side without being told; it is now automatic for him.

One park in particular I take him to has walkways that go in various directions and I decided to try something I had never thought of with any other dog. I wanted to see if he would understand different commands, such as right, left, straight, wait, stop, go, go across, and turn around. I had an added problem here and that was squirrels. All training stops when they are around. I cease to exist when squirrels appear and he hears not one word I say.

I asked Frank to go to this particular park with me one day so I could demonstrate Tyler's great prowess with these commands. Needless to say, Frank expressed surprise and admiration when Tyler showed his great abilities. It was great fun to see Frank's surprise as Tyler completed each command.

It is at times like this that I think, "What a shame his previous owners would never realize the great potential and intelligence that we have been able to experience."

Most of all, I thank God that He chose us to take care of one of His precious creatures. He knew just who to pick for this privilege.

"When the Man waked up he said, 'What is Wild Dog doing here?'

And the Woman said, 'His name is not Wild Dog any more,

but the First Friend, because he will be our friend

for always and always and always.'"

- Rudyard Kipling

A DOG NEVER

GIVES JUST

PART OF HIS

HEART - HE GIVES IT

ALL

We are certain that Tyler was abused and mistreated prior to receiving the injuries to his mouth. He has never overcome his fear of all loud noises. He is fearful if something makes a loud noise when it is dropped or tossed away.   Tyler will leave the kitchen and hide under the dining room table when ice comes out of the ice dispenser on the front door of the refrigerator.

Unfortunately, there is a gun range close to his favorite park that has nice long trails and huge century old trees. He loves to be in the park until the sounds of shots in the distance frightens him and makes him want to leave immediately.   Tyler still enjoys going to this park when there is no shooting. We live approximately two or three miles due north of this range. When there is shooting and the wind is strong from the south, Tyler scrambles for the door when he is outside.

The 4th of July has become much worse and even more frightening for him. As a result, Dr. Baker has given him sedatives; however, the sedatives seem to have little effect on him. My heart breaks for him.

We have even prayed over him, but bad memories seem to override everything in his psyche. All we can do is hold him and let him know we love him and that we are there.

Tyler knows we would never intentionally hurt him. As a result, he lets us and the vet do whatever is necessary. He seems to know we only want to help him. Whether he is probed, prodded or injected, he just allows us to complete the procedure. He is secure in the knowledge that we love him and will not harm him. He gifts us with an unusual level of trust that is deeply rooted and based on mutual love. If I do accidentally hurt him, I immediately stop and lean down by his face and say, "I am sorry." Tyler then snuggles his face into my neck and melts. He will stay there to let me know he truly understands that it was an accident. This is his way of letting me know everything is okay between us. It is so precious and again shows us how Tyler shares his heart with us.

When Tyler comes to one of us with a look of excitement, we ask him, "What do you want? Show me." He continues to do just that! Sometimes he looks at the back door as if to tell us he wants to go outside. At other times, he goes near the kitchen cabinet where his treats are kept with a pleading look before breaking into his dance for goodies.

Tyler is a very polite dog and has an uncanny sense in knowing when a situation requires politeness and delicacy. He can be very excitable, yet when it is necessary to stay away from a situation, he will either go under the dining room table or go upstairs. He will stay there until the crisis is over.

There have been times during high tension events that Tyler will come up behind me and will nudge the backs of my knees. When he does this, it is his wonderful way of saying, "Hey, mom, chill out." It's his way of letting me know he is always there for me.

Another interesting fact about his politeness is that I have never accidentally stepped on him or tripped over him. Even if I am not aware of his proximity to me, he seems to know exactly where I am. He always stays close to the wall if we are in the hallway or a tight area, but his instinct is to always stay one step behind me. This is the herding instinct attributable to his breed. It always seems that Tyler is watching out for me.

Tyler responds to one command as if he knows that at some point, it could be of paramount importance that this command is followed. I have never had a dog who responded to this command. The command is, "Go get daddy." Frank and I have discussed that when Tyler comes to us with his expectant eyes as if he is pleading with us, we will stop what we are doing to go see if the other person needs help. In our house, if we are in different areas of the house, just raising your voice to call out to the other person serves no purpose – you do not hear them calling. Tyler obeys this command quickly and has never failed to follow through. If Tyler was a human, he would definitely be called a gentleman of the highest degree.

Speaking of being a gentleman, I have tried to get him to do certain things, but if he does not feel right about it, he will not do it. For instance, one time I put his favorite dog biscuit between my teeth for him to take from me. To my utter surprise, he walked away and made no attempt to get the dog biscuit. It's as if he knows that if his teeth are close by my face, there is the possibility of him accidentally hurting me. What a guy!! There is no other instance when Tyler ever turns down a dog biscuit! He looks for reasons to get them as often as possible.

There are countless stories that tell about a dog's devotion to their owners and we have seen that first hand with Tyler.

You also often hear that dogs can sense when their owners are ill or out of sorts. Tyler's devotion and his sensitivity became readily apparent when I became ill in March 2012. As a result of this illness, I slept for three days with no particular symptoms, not knowing that my body was reacting to a change in my medication. It was very strange to say the least.

As I was asleep, I had no way of knowing that a special furry "angel" watched over me for the whole three days. Yes, as Frank told me later, Tyler stayed in the bedroom almost the entire time – just watching me.

It warmed my heart to know that Tyler somehow "knew" and that he stayed close to me. All those stories I had heard for years about dogs and how they showed their love actually happened to me!

"My little dog---a heartbeat at my feet."

- Edith Wharton

HOW DOES HE

DO THAT??!?

There was never a single dog that I had previously owned that knew the names of other people. It's as if introductions are made and Tyler files the name in his own little memory bank. He only has to hear a name once or twice and from that point forward, he seems to know exactly who I am talking about. Our youngest son, Trevor and his wife, Laura, had been over a just few times after Tyler came to live with us. As Tyler was still overflowing with that puppy exuberance, he loved it when Trevor wrestled around with him. One evening when they were planning to be at our house, I told Tyler that Trevor and Laura were coming. He immediately went into his excitement mode when he heard their names. I finally told Tyler he could sit on front porch and wait for them. I very explicitly told him he was not allowed to leave the porch. When Trevor and Laura arrived about 15-20 minutes later, there was Tyler still on the porch waiting for them! There have been so many instances since that evening when Tyler patiently sat waiting that have proven he knows the people we are talking about. This particular instance made such an impact on me because he was still quite young and I had never had a dog that seemed to know the names of people.

One of my favorite incidents happened during the summer and it still makes me chuckle. I mentioned earlier how Tyler considers it a personal challenge to chase every rabbit and squirrel and if Tyler could talk, he would tell you it is his absolute favorite thing to do. One summer at dusk, he had that chance. I was at the front door and Tyler was right beside me. Suddenly, he spotted a rabbit two houses away. He took off at warp speed and I figured that I had seen the last of him until bedtime. The only thing that popped into my mind to say to get him to come back was, "No walk." Tyler heard me say "No walk." in my most stern voice. Our neighbor was watching and we were both in total shock when Tyler suddenly stopped on a dime. He turned around and came right back.

It was as if Tyler decided instantly that a walk certainly trumps a rabbit or squirrel! Such a fun moment! It made me think of a child when they misbehave and, as a result, they are not allowed to have a treat or a certain privilege.

We came to find out soon after bringing Tyler home that he understood a lot more than we realized. His vocabulary rapidly increased to the point that we needed to spell many things, especially the things he likes. We quickly resorted to spelling such words as walk, go in the car, peanut butter, popcorn or treats.

He also understands some of our sentences, especially if they include references to him. We have learned that we cannot even refer to "him" or "dog" because Tyler knows we're talking about him. We may have to resort to writing notes to each other!

"You do not own a dog,

the dog owns you."

- Unknown

EVERY DAY

REALLY IS A

GIFT

We were sitting at home one Sunday evening just channel surfing to see what was on TV. The ex-governor Mike Huckabee was interviewing a man and wife regarding "God-encounters and how He sets us up for circumstances that benefit us." As Christians, we know this as a fact, but many call it "dumb luck" and don't realize He deserves the credit for divine-encounters. The couple shared a story that was so amazing that had it not been His hand in the situation, it would never have happened without Him. As they were talking, I had this "knowing" in me that I would soon be having an experience such as this. Of course, I had no idea when or where it would be, but it happened the very next day!

On the following day, I decided to take Tyler to one of the parks closer to our house.

As we started out on our walk, I quickly noticed a lady and her black dog. The dog was trotting along and the dog and its owner kept a safe distance from us. We were both there for the same length of time and when Tyler and I finished, she and her dog were also ready to go. I kept my eye on her to see where she was headed with her dog and something prompted me to take note. As I kept watching, I felt as if the Lord wanted me to ask her about the type of dog she had and information about the breeding.

After getting in the car and driving around to where she was walking, I called to her and asked if she knew the breed of her dog. She responded that her dog was part Labrador and part Border Collie. I told her that Tyler was a black Labrador mix. He seemed to be mixed with a herding breed, but we had never known any more about which herding breed. The two dogs were remarkably similar in appearance except that Tyler did not have a tail and the other dog had a normal looking long Labrador tail. When the other dog turned and looked at me I knew: this is Tyler's breeding also!

When Frank came home, I told him about meeting this lady with the dog who looked like Tyler. We quickly got online to look up this breed mixture and found the description of the Labrador Collie breed which almost exactly fit Tyler. The photos show a very close match to Tyler's face without the white on it because Tyler is almost totally black. I was praising God's intervention that day. What a gift to have the knowledge and be able to read about Tyler's breed. Our wondering about his breeding was over. We always knew Tyler owned his own space in our hearts and we now knew more about his whole breed.

After having found this article about a Labrador Collie mix, I realized how true the statement was about "remarkably easy to train." When we first got him, we took him to puppy training class and it proved to be true. However, when we left his "classroom" and it came to training him, all bets were off for certain commands. When it came to the word "Heel, " he would at first obey, but he would last no further than about twenty feet. For some reason, this command was not one he chose to obey. It seems as if he just cannot stand to be so restricted. All other training has been amazingly easy and he quickly picks up commands.

One of the reasons I felt Tyler had a herding breed in him was because of his joy of running for the sheer love of it. When we take him to his favorite park, which is at least a quarter mile in length, we remove his leash. He immediately takes off and you can almost see the smile on his face as he runs the length of the park. It takes him only sixteen seconds to go that distance. It is phenomenal!

Watching Tyler run is reminiscent of watching a western movie when the cattle or sheep dog is running at top speed on the outside of the herd, keeping the herd together and ensuring there are no strays. Dr. Baker told us when we first took him home that we would experience him herding us and this has become very clear to see. It points again to the particular breed in him. As he loves running so much, regardless of the heat in summer, he seems to drink gallons of water. We always make sure we have plenty on hand. Also, being black in color probably intensifies the heat for him.

The wonderful thing about having Tyler is that it seems there is something new every day. Often times, it is not at all what we might be expecting! He absolutely never fails to amaze us, especially when he comes to conclusions of the circumstances either he is in or that he sees us in. There are times that no words are necessary, he just knows what to do and he does it.

No one has to tell him. I am sure other dogs are capable of this ability to look at entire situations and react in the proper way, but to be honest; I either never noticed it or never realized it existed in previous dogs.

"Dogs are our link to paradise. They don't know evil or jealousy or discontent. To sit with a dog on a hillside on a glorious afternoon is to be back in Eden, where doing nothing was not boring--it was peace."

- Milan Kundera

LIFE GOES

ON......

THANKFULLY

I am so blessed by how encouraging people have been about wanting me to write about Tyler. As I start wrapping this up, I know Tyler will always be doing more and more spectacular things. It always seems to be the case with him. As these events occur, even though they won't make it into this book, they will be forever tucked away in our hearts.

I am sure many people have experienced what we have with Tyler, with their own dogs; however, it is such a new and wonderful experience for us that I had to share with you our lives with Tyler.

There are still so many things I know I could tell you about him, but before I finish you must meet his "babies."

Tyler has a few squeaky toys that are usually under the dining room table. When I first gave them to him, I referred to them as "your babies." Let me introduce you to them. "Dottie" is a Dalmatian puppy. "Yellow dog" is a circle, attached at head and tail. "Karate" is in his karate uniform. "Pinkie" is a pink, little puppy with its tongue sticking out. Finally, there is "Fishy," a fish with gills along its sides who makes a gurgling sound when squeezed.

Tyler loves his little critters and will go under the table and start squeaking one of his babies to get my attention. I always respond because I know Tyler feels that he needs some attention. It's as if I am playing with a toddler. I sit down by the table and talk for the animals and squeeze them. We play just like you would with a child and he loves it. The sweet thing is he squeezes them just enough to make them squeak. The only one he's ever torn open is Karate. It is a recurring injury for Karate's leg to be hanging by a thread with stuffing coming out. I just shove it back in and a few days later I will see little tufts laying around again and we start all over again!

For Christmas 2012, Tyler received two new babies. "Squeaky" is a cute little hedgehog. He also received a duck in flight that makes a honking sound. When I gave them to Tyler, he was beyond excited! He knew immediately they were his. When I started squeezing them, their own distinctive sounds seemed to excite him even more! It was so cute to watch. I had so much fun giving him new babies that I know I will be doing it more often than just at Christmas!

We take Tyler to a local store where a very kind lady, Linda, and her staff have been angels in their grooming of Tyler for over three years. Linda told us that on the first visit, Tyler was very difficult to bathe. He especially disliked being put in a kennel after he was bathed and blown dry. As each month came and went, he seemed to be calmer each time he was groomed. Now, even though I can see him quivering on the drive to the store, Tyler is actually impatient and can't wait to see Linda. He reacts the same way he does at Dr. Baker's office. He goes in and plants his front feet up on the counter to greet her. Recently, Linda said, "Tyler is my major success story." It had been so stressful for us the first few times Tyler was groomed that we almost stopped taking him. Now we are so glad we didn't give up. In early times, Tyler would never stand still to be brushed. The type of brush we used helped remove loose hair. After Linda and her staff patiently took care of his grooming, he now understands what we need to do. He stands perfectly still to allow us to brush him. I also have to mention his beautiful shiny black coat and how people always comment on it. The photographs in this book show what a handsome dog he is.

This brings you up to date as to where we are now, well into the year 2013. Tyler is into his fifth year of life with new adventures surely to come.

There are several retired Agents who are really looking forward to hearing about "our" Tyler which prompted me to write this book. Thanks to them and their kind hearts, Tyler is with us today.

I have so enjoyed looking back at his adventures and knowing he still has many years ahead of him which I am sure will include more amazing things. All I can say to you is that it has been an honor that our heavenly Father chose us to care for one of His precious creatures.

Sometimes there are spaces in your life that exist and you don't even realize it. God knew that Tyler would fit perfectly in our lives. In fact, it would be hard to imagine our lives without the space that is Tyler. We know he was not only sent to us, but meant to be with us. He has shown us so much about patience, never giving up and how beautifully love works. What a gift Tyler is!

At the beginning of this book, Tyler's story began with the age-old phrase of "Once upon a time……" Therefore, it is only fitting that at the end of the book, you should know that Tyler is indeed living happily ever after!

"He is your friend, your partner, your defender, your dog. He will be yours, faithful and true, to the last beat of his heart. You owe it to him to be worthy of such devotion."

EPILOGUE

In regards to Tyler, when I think of the very last paragraph in John 21: 25, it reminds me of how many fun things Tyler has done and all the human words he understands. The only way I would be able to tell you would be to have written down those things that occurred every hour of every day. The verse above says: "And there are also many other things that Jesus did, which if they were written one by one, I suppose that even the world itself could not contain the books that would be written. Amen." (NKJV)

ABOUT THE

BREED

The Lab Collie mix is probably one of, if not the most loyal breed of dog you will ever have the good fortune to come across.   Not only are they loyal, but both Labradors and Border Collies are incredibly intelligent and have great temperaments.

All of these traits make them perfect family dogs. They are lovable and playful and are also very eager to please their owners.

Collies are very athletic and have great endurance, but a Lab Collie mix is slightly less energetic as well as being slightly less intense. This makes them brilliant for an owner who wants a Collie, but cannot dedicate as much time or energy to them.

Both Labs and Collies are well known for their superb herding and retrieving qualities, so if you have lost your keys, this dog will be able to help you find them! They are remarkably easy to train because for generations, Collies have been bred to fulfill a useful role alongside men.   This explains why they are so obedient.

If this dog is trained as a puppy, it will become a

very hard worker. It will also prove to be hugely rewarding to any owner, whether it's within a family or not. As a result, you will find that they are house-trained very easily and, if given enough attention, will not get to grips with any of your furniture or mess up any of your floors!

Not only is the Lab Collie mix obedient and very easily trained, they are also a bundle of fun and will provide any owner with hours of entertainment. They do not need as much exercise as purebred Collies, but still need quite a bit. Obviously, the more exercise they get, the more beneficial it will be to their health.

Experts believe that this breed of dog is one of the best working dogs in the world. Lab Collies have become very popular with families and there is often a rather long waiting list for puppies. You should put your name down as soon as you decide to get one of these lovely dogs. Otherwise, you could be in for a disappointing wait!

To ensure that this breed of dog fits in with the family, it needs to be socialized at a young age. This will prevent shyness later on in their lives. As long as this animal has enough attention, exercise and a "job" to do, as such, it will be perfectly happy within any household. They are medium-sized dogs, so should not take over your entire house. They are also medium-haired dogs and only need a minimal amount of grooming. However, you should make sure that the hair does not get tangled and the dog should be checked out at the vet as with any other breed of dog.

All in all, a Lab Collie mix would be perfect for you if you want a playful, energetic dog that has bundles of love to give and is easily trained.

Stephanie L King

ABOUT THE AUTHOR

Stephanie L. King is a mother of two sons and grandmother of four grandchildren. She was ordained as a Reverend in 2004 and has counseled numerous people dealing with a variety of issues. As Stephanie has always been a lover of animals, especially horses and dogs, she has enjoyed her first endeavor in writing this book. With Tyler as the topic, it made it a much simpler effort. Stephanie attended Mt. San Antonio Jr. College in Walnut, CA.

Stephanie met her husband, Frank, at the FBI Office in Los Angeles, California in 1967 where they both served as clerks. When Frank became an Agent, they moved to his first office assignment in Oklahoma City, Oklahoma.

Stephanie currently resides in Northeastern Oklahoma with her husband and with the rest of her family close by. She can be reached via email at slk@reagan.com.

Stephanie L King

I Want You To Call Him Tyler

Made in the USA
Charleston, SC
24 May 2013